HOW TO INVEST FOR BEGINNERS

A Comprehensive Guide from $10,000 to a Million and Beyond

Jerry R. Schaefer

TABLE OF CONTENTS

Chapter 1: Foundation for Financial Growth

Embark on your journey from $10,000 to a million by establishing a robust financial foundation. This chapter unveils the critical importance of tackling high-interest debt as the first step towards prosperity. Dive into insightful strategies for paying off credit card and consumer debt, paving the way for sustainable financial growth. Lay the groundwork for success as we explore the fundamental principles that will shape your wealth-building journey. Gain a clear understanding of the impact of debt on your financial goals and equip yourself with practical tools to eliminate obstacles on the path to becoming a millionaire.

Introduction to the Journey from $10,000 to a Million

Welcome to the transformative journey of turning $10,000 into a million dollars—a voyage not just of financial ascent but a holistic journey toward prosperity. In a world saturated with financial advice, this guide is a beacon, steering you through practical steps and strategic decisions. As you embark on this expedition, envision a future where your financial dreams become reality.

Setting the Stage

At the outset, it's crucial to acknowledge that this journey is not a get-rich-quick scheme. It's a disciplined approach to wealth-building, grounded in thoughtful actions and informed decisions. The $10,000 represents your seed capital, and the million is the tangible result of calculated moves and transformative financial habits.

The Power of Starting Small

Why start with $10,000? It's a sum attainable for many, making the journey relatable and accessible. Whether you've diligently saved or received an unexpected windfall, this guide is designed for those who understand the potential within even a modest starting point. The journey from $10,000 symbolizes the empowerment of individuals to grow wealth systematically.

Unveiling the Roadmap

The roadmap unfolds across seven chapters, each meticulously crafted to address key aspects of financial growth. As we navigate through these chapters, you'll encounter insights, strategies, and real-life examples that demystify the process of turning a seemingly modest amount into a substantial fortune.

Your Journey Begins Now

This guide isn't just about reaching a numerical milestone; it's about empowerment, informed decisions, and the evolution of your financial mindset. Embrace the journey, apply the principles, and witness the transformation of $10,000 into a million—a testament to the remarkable potential within us all. Your odyssey to financial prosperity starts now.

Understanding the Impact of High-Interest Debt

Debt, especially in the form of high-interest loans and credit card balances, is a formidable adversary on the path to financial prosperity. In this chapter, we unravel the intricate web woven by these financial burdens and delve into the profound impact they can have on your journey from $10,000 to a million.

The Weight of Interest

High-interest debt carries an inherent weight that can stifle even the most ambitious financial goals. As your debt accumulates, so does the interest, creating a compounding effect that can feel insurmountable. What might start as a seemingly manageable sum can quickly snowball into a substantial obstacle, hindering your ability to allocate resources toward wealth-building endeavors?

Erosion of Income

One of the insidious effects of high-interest debt is the erosion of your income. A significant portion of your hard-earned money is redirected towards servicing debt rather than contributing to your financial growth. This relentless drain on your income limits your capacity to save, invest, or engage in opportunities that could propel you toward your million-dollar goal.

Impaired Creditworthiness

Beyond the immediate financial strain, high-interest debt can tarnish your creditworthiness. A lower credit score may lead to higher interest rates on future loans, perpetuating a cycle of financial disadvantage. Understanding this ripple effect is crucial; repairing your credit is not only about current debt but also about positioning yourself for future financial success.

Emotional Toll

The impact of high-interest debt extends beyond the tangible financial consequences, reaching into the realm of emotional well-being. The stress and anxiety associated with looming debt can take a toll on mental health, affecting decision-making and overall life satisfaction. This emotional burden becomes a silent but formidable adversary, hindering the clarity and focus needed for strategic financial planning.

Shackles on Financial Freedom

Consider high-interest debt as shackles constraining your financial freedom. Breaking free from these chains is not only a practical necessity but also a symbolic act of reclaiming control over your financial destiny. By understanding the true cost of carrying this burden, you empower yourself to make informed decisions and embark on a transformative journey toward financial liberation.

The Road to Liberation

As we navigate through the impact of high-interest debt, the narrative shifts towards liberation. This chapter is not just about highlighting the challenges but providing a roadmap for overcoming them. Strategies for debt elimination, negotiation with creditors, and prudent financial management become the tools for breaking free from the entanglements of high-interest debt.

Crafting a Debt-Elimination Plan

Crafting a debt-elimination plan is the cornerstone of your journey. Assessing the total debt, prioritizing high-interest balances, and exploring consolidation options are pivotal steps. By creating a systematic plan tailored to your financial situation, you initiate the process of dismantling the financial barriers that stand between you and your million-dollar goal.

Negotiating with Creditors

Effective communication with creditors can be a powerful tool in your debt-elimination toolkit. Many creditors are open to negotiation, offering possibilities such as interest rate reductions, debt settlements, or revised repayment terms. This chapter provides practical insights into approaching these conversations, transforming what may seem like an adversarial relationship into a collaborative effort toward financial recovery.

Prudent Financial Management

Beyond debt elimination, adopting prudent financial management practices is essential for sustained success. This includes budgeting, building an emergency fund, and cultivating disciplined spending habits. As you implement these strategies, you fortify your financial foundation, ensuring that once liberated from high-interest debt, you remain on a trajectory toward lasting prosperity.

A Liberated Future

Understanding the impact of high-interest debt is the first step towards liberation. This chapter equips you with the knowledge to navigate the complexities of debt and lays the groundwork for your financial emancipation. As you embark on the subsequent chapters, envision a future unburdened by the weight of high-interest debt—a future where your financial resources are directed towards wealth-building endeavors, propelling you closer to the million-dollar milestone. The journey to financial freedom begins with the liberation from debt, setting the stage for a transformative expedition ahead.

Strategies for Paying Off Credit Card and Consumer Debt

Escaping the clutches of high-interest debt demands strategic planning and disciplined execution. In this chapter, we'll delve into actionable strategies specifically tailored to liberate you from the burdens of credit card and consumer debt. By understanding these strategies, you not only regain control of your finances but also set the stage for the robust foundation needed to propel your journey from $10,000 to a million.

1. Snowball vs. Avalanche Method

Two prominent methods for tackling multiple debts are the snowball and avalanche methods. The snowball method involves paying off the smallest debts first, gaining momentum as you move to larger ones. On the other hand, the avalanche method prioritizes debts with the highest interest rates, minimizing overall interest paid. Choose the method that aligns with your psychological and financial preferences.

2. Budgeting Mastery

Creating a comprehensive budget is paramount in debt elimination. Evaluate your income, categorize expenses, and identify areas where you can cut back. The surplus funds can be redirected towards debt repayment. This disciplined budgeting approach not only accelerates debt reduction but also instills financial habits crucial for future wealth-building endeavors.

3. Negotiating Interest Rates

Engage with your creditors to negotiate lower interest rates. Many credit card companies are open to such discussions, especially if you have a history of on-time payments. A reduced interest rate can significantly alleviate the financial strain, enabling more of your payments to go toward the principal amount.

4. Debt Consolidation

Consolidating multiple debts into a single, lower-interest loan is a powerful strategy. This simplifies repayment by streamlining multiple payments into one, potentially reducing the overall interest burden. However, exercise caution and thoroughly assess the terms of the consolidation to ensure it genuinely benefits your financial situation.

5. Windfall Allocation

Unexpected windfalls, such as tax refunds or work bonuses, present golden opportunities to make substantial debt payments. Rather than allocating these funds elsewhere, consider directing them towards high-interest debt. This accelerates the repayment process, providing a substantial leap forward on your journey to financial freedom.

6. Emergency Fund Establishment

While it may seem counterintuitive, building an emergency fund is crucial for sustained debt repayment. Without a financial safety net, unexpected expenses could force you to revert to credit for survival. By establishing an emergency fund, you create a buffer, reducing the reliance on credit and allowing you to stay on track with your debt-elimination plan.

7. Credit Counseling and Debt Management Plans

Seeking professional guidance through credit counseling can offer valuable insights into your financial situation. Credit counselors can help negotiate with creditors, provide budgeting advice, and potentially enroll you in a debt management plan. These plans involve consolidating debts and negotiating lower interest rates, offering a structured path toward debt elimination.

8. Mindful Spending Habits

Address the root cause of consumer debt by cultivating mindful spending habits. Differentiate between needs and wants, prioritize essential expenses, and cut out discretionary spending. This shift in mindset not only aids in debt repayment but fosters a sustainable approach to managing finances in the long term.

9. Celebrating Milestones

Celebrate small victories along the way. Whether it's paying off a particular debt or reaching a specific milestone, acknowledging your progress fosters motivation. This positive reinforcement strengthens your commitment to the debt repayment journey, making it more likely that you'll persist in the face of challenges.

10. Continuous Monitoring and Adjustment

Financial circumstances evolve, and so should your debt-elimination strategy. Regularly monitor your progress, assess your budget, and adjust your repayment plan as needed. This adaptability ensures that your approach remains aligned with your current financial situation, maximizing its effectiveness.

Liberating Yourself from Debt

By incorporating these strategies into your debt-elimination plan, you empower yourself to break free from the shackles of credit card and consumer debt. The journey to a million dollars starts with liberating your income from the grip of high-interest debt, laying the groundwork for a future where your financial resources are channeled towards wealth-building endeavors. As you apply these strategies, envision a debt-free horizon—a crucial milestone on your transformative path to financial prosperity.

Chapter 2: Real Estate Wealth Creation

Unlock the potential of real estate as a catalyst for your journey from $10,000 to a million. Explore the benefits of acquiring a primary residence with a 3% down payment, demystifying the world of real estate investment. From strategic property selection to leveraging market trends, this chapter provides the insights needed to harness the power of real estate on your path to substantial wealth creation. Embrace the opportunities within this tangible asset class, as we guide you through the transformative landscape of real estate wealth building.

Leveraging Real Estate for Financial Growth

Real estate stands as an enduring cornerstone of wealth creation, offering a tangible and resilient avenue for financial growth. In this chapter, we embark on a journey into the dynamic realm of real estate, exploring how strategic leveraging can propel you from $10,000 to a million.

The Power of Real Assets

Real estate, unlike many other investments, provides a tangible asset—one you can see, touch, and inhabit. This inherent physicality imparts a sense of stability and permanence, making real estate a valuable component in any diversified investment portfolio. The potential for both appreciation and regular income streams positions real estate as a versatile wealth-building tool.

Acquiring a Primary Residence

The gateway to real estate wealth creation often begins with acquiring a primary residence. What sets this strategy apart is the ability to make a substantial investment with a minimal down payment—sometimes as low as 3%. This accessibility allows individuals with modest starting capital, like the $10,000 in our scenario, to enter the real estate market and benefit from potential property appreciation over time.

Building Equity through Mortgage Payments

The magic of leveraging in real estate is evident in the mechanism of mortgage payments. As you contribute towards your mortgage, each payment simultaneously reduces debt and builds equity. Over time, this dual effect contributes to the growth of your net worth. The principle of leveraging, where you use borrowed funds to increase the potential return on investment, comes to life as your property appreciates while your mortgage balance decreases.

The Appreciation Advantage

Real estate has historically demonstrated the potential for appreciation. The value of properties tends to increase over time, influenced by factors such as location, economic trends, and development in the vicinity. While short-term fluctuations may occur, a judiciously chosen property, especially in high-demand areas, can be a powerful wealth-building asset.

Rental Income as a Revenue Stream

Beyond mere appreciation, rental income further enhances the financial allure of real estate. By strategically purchasing properties with rental potential, you transform your real estate holdings into revenue-generating assets. This not only aids in covering mortgage payments but also contributes to your overall income, laying the groundwork for financial stability and growth.

Tax Advantages in Real Estate

Real estate investment offers a spectrum of tax advantages, further augmenting its appeal. Deductions for mortgage interest, property taxes, and certain expenses can significantly reduce your taxable income. Understanding and leveraging these tax benefits becomes an integral part of optimizing the financial advantages associated with real estate.

Mitigating Risks through Diversification

While real estate presents lucrative opportunities, prudent investors also consider risk mitigation. Diversification within real estate, such as owning different types of properties or investing in diverse geographical locations, helps spread risk. This thoughtful approach safeguards your portfolio against localized market fluctuations, enhancing the resilience of your real estate investments.

Scaling Up with Additional Properties

Once you've experienced success with your primary residence, scaling up by acquiring additional properties becomes a strategic move. The equity built into the initial property can be leveraged to secure financing for subsequent investments. This progression allows you to diversify your real estate holdings and multiply the potential for wealth creation.

Strategic Property Selection

Not all real estate is created equal, and strategic property selection is paramount. Factors such as location, market trends, and potential for development play pivotal roles. Research and due diligence are essential, ensuring that your investments align with your long-term financial goals. This chapter provides insights into recognizing properties poised for appreciation and rental income.

Navigating the Real Estate Landscape

As we navigate the expansive landscape of leveraging real estate for financial growth, envision a future where your real assets act as dynamic catalysts for wealth creation. This chapter serves as a guide, imparting the knowledge and strategies needed to harness the power of real estate on your journey from $10,000 to a million. Embrace the potential within this tangible asset class, and let the appreciation and income streams from real estate become key contributors to your transformative financial ascent.

Benefits of Buying a Primary Residence with a 3% Down Payment

Investing in real estate often begins with the pivotal decision to buy a primary residence, and opting for a low down payment can be a strategic move that propels you closer to financial success. In this chapter, we explore the myriad benefits of purchasing a primary residence with a 3% down payment, demystifying the path to real estate wealth creation from your initial investment of $10,000.

1. Accessibility for Modest Capital

The primary advantage of a 3% down payment is accessibility. For individuals with a limited initial capital, such as the $10,000 in our scenario, this option opens the doors to homeownership and real estate investment. Traditional down payments often require 20% or more, creating a significant barrier for those looking to enter the market. With a 3% down payment, the threshold for entry becomes much more attainable.

2. Preservation of Capital

Opting for a lower down payment allows you to preserve a substantial portion of your initial capital. This preserved capital can be strategically allocated toward other wealth-building endeavors or serve as a financial buffer. It ensures that you have liquidity available for emergencies, investments, or future opportunities that may arise on your journey from $10,000 to a million.

3. Immediate Homeownership Benefits

A 3% down payment expedites the process of transitioning from renting to homeownership. Rather than waiting years to accumulate a larger down payment, you can seize the immediate benefits of owning a home. These include stability, control over your living space, and potential tax advantages. The sooner you enter the real estate market, the sooner you begin building equity and leveraging the value of your property.

4. Leveraging Mortgage Financing

Low down payments leverage the power of mortgage financing. By using borrowed funds for a significant portion of the property's purchase price, you magnify your potential returns. Mortgage payments contribute to both reducing debt and building equity simultaneously. This leveraging effect becomes a catalyst for wealth creation as your property appreciates over time.

5. Potential for Property Appreciation

Real estate, historically, has shown the potential for appreciation. While not guaranteed, purchasing a primary residence in a location with promising growth prospects enhances the likelihood of your property appreciating. This appreciation, when combined with your lower initial investment, can yield substantial returns on your capital.

6. Building Equity with Mortgage Payments

Each mortgage payment made is a step towards building equity in your property. With a 3% down payment, you initiate this process sooner. As you make regular payments, a larger portion goes towards reducing the principal amount owed. This equity accumulation becomes a valuable asset, contributing to your overall net worth and providing financial flexibility.

7. Stable Housing Costs

By securing a primary residence with a fixed-rate mortgage, you gain the advantage of stable housing costs. Unlike renting, where landlords can increase rent at their discretion, your mortgage payments remain consistent throughout the loan term. This stability facilitates better long-term financial planning and ensures that your housing costs do not spiral out of control.

8. Potential for Rental Income

Another benefit of purchasing a primary residence is the potential for rental income. As life circumstances change, you might choose to move but retain ownership of your property. Renting out your primary residence can generate additional income streams, contributing to mortgage payments or serving as a source of passive income.

9. Tax Deductions and Credits

Homeownership often brings about tax advantages. Mortgage interest deductions, property tax deductions, and potential first-time homebuyer credits can significantly reduce your overall tax liability. These financial perks add to the appeal of purchasing a primary residence, enhancing the overall return on investment.

10. Setting the Stage for Future Investments

Choosing a primary residence with a 3% down payment is not just about immediate benefits; it's about setting the stage for future investments. The equity built in your primary residence becomes a valuable asset that can be leveraged for subsequent real estate endeavors. This strategic progression allows you to scale up your real estate portfolio, moving you closer to the million-dollar milestone.

Envisioning Real Estate Wealth

In embracing the benefits of buying a primary residence with a 3% down payment, you set the tone for your real estate wealth creation journey. This chapter serves as a compass, guiding you through the advantages of this strategic approach and illustrating how your initial investment of $10,000 can burgeon into a robust real estate portfolio. Embrace the potential, seize the benefits, and envision a future where your primary residence becomes a cornerstone of your financial prosperity.

Selecting the Right Property for Potential Appreciation

In the intricate dance of real estate investment, the choice of the right property becomes a pivotal decision that can significantly impact your journey from $10,000 to a million. This chapter unravels the nuanced art of selecting a property poised for potential appreciation, delving into key considerations and strategies that elevate your real estate investment game.

Location, Location, Location

The timeless adage in real estate—location matters—resonates profoundly when seeking potential appreciation. A strategic location not only ensures immediate desirability but also anticipates future growth. Consider factors such as proximity to employment hubs, quality of schools, local amenities, and infrastructure development. A location with a positive outlook ensures your property is positioned for long-term value appreciation.

Market Trends and Economic Indicators

Understanding market trends and economic indicators is akin to reading the pulse of real estate. Research the historical performance of the area and identify patterns in property value appreciation. Economic stability, job growth, and population trends are key indicators. A region with a flourishing economy is likely to attract sustained demand for real estate, fostering a conducive environment for appreciation.

Development and Infrastructure Plans

Keep an eye on municipal development plans and infrastructure projects. Areas undergoing revitalization or slated for significant infrastructure improvements often experience an uptick in property values. New transportation links, parks, and commercial developments contribute to the overall appeal of a location, making it a potential hotspot for real estate appreciation.

Neighborhood Dynamics

Zoom in on the microcosm of neighborhood dynamics. A property's potential for appreciation is intricately tied to the characteristics of its surroundings. Evaluate the overall condition of neighboring properties, crime rates, and community amenities. A vibrant and well-maintained neighborhood enhances the appeal of your property, positively influencing its potential for future appreciation.

School District Quality

The quality of local schools is a critical factor for both current desirability and future appreciation. Families often prioritize proximity to quality educational institutions, influencing property demand. Research the reputation of schools in the area and understand their impact on property values. A property in a coveted school district is more likely to experience sustained appreciation.

Historical Appreciation Data

Examine historical appreciation data for the specific property and surrounding area. Patterns of past performance can offer insights into potential future trends. Real estate analytics and historical sales data provide a comprehensive picture of how properties in the vicinity have appreciated over time, guiding your decision-making process.

Supply and Demand Dynamics

The fundamental principles of supply and demand play a crucial role in real estate appreciation. Evaluate the supply of properties in the area relative to the demand. A market where demand outstrips supply often leads to increased property values. Conversely, an oversaturated market may limit appreciation potential. Analyzing these dynamics helps you gauge the future trajectory of property values.

Potential for Urbanization

Urbanization trends can significantly influence real estate appreciation. Areas experiencing urban development or transformation into business hubs tend to witness increased property values. Identify regions with potential for urbanization, as this often correlates with heightened demand and, consequently, appreciation in property values.

Future Zoning and Land Use

Research future zoning and land use regulations in the area. Changes in zoning can impact the potential uses of nearby properties, affecting their value. Stay informed about upcoming zoning amendments and land use plans that may enhance the appeal and value of your chosen property.

Consultation with Real Estate Professionals

Engaging with local real estate professionals can provide invaluable insights. Real estate agents, property appraisers, and market analysts possess on-the-ground knowledge that complements your research. Their expertise can guide you in identifying properties with the highest potential for appreciation, aligning with your investment goals.

Risk Mitigation Strategies

While seeking potential appreciation is paramount, prudent investors also consider risk mitigation. Diversifying your real estate portfolio, maintaining liquidity, and staying informed about external factors that could impact property values are crucial risk management strategies. A well-rounded approach ensures resilience in the face of unforeseen challenges.

The Holistic Approach to Selection

Selecting the right property for potential appreciation involves weaving together these considerations into a holistic approach. It's not just about the property itself but understanding its context within the broader real estate landscape. This chapter serves as a guide, equipping you with the knowledge and tools needed to make informed decisions that position your property for future appreciation.

Envisioning Future Wealth

As you navigate the landscape of selecting the right property for potential appreciation, envision a future where your real estate investments flourish and contribute significantly to your financial ascent. This chapter is a compass, guiding you through the intricacies of property selection, and empowering you to make choices that align with your vision of reaching the million-dollar milestone through strategic real estate wealth creation. Embrace the possibilities, and let the right property become a cornerstone of your transformative journey.

Chapter 3: Entrepreneurial Ventures

Embark on the exhilarating path of entrepreneurial ventures as a key pillar on your journey from $10,000 to a million. This chapter unravels the transformative potential of acquiring small businesses, paying royalties to local owners, and navigating the entrepreneurial landscape. Explore the intricacies of due diligence, negotiation, and strategic management, unlocking the door to exponential financial growth through savvy business acquisitions. As we delve into the world of entrepreneurship, envision a future where your ventures contribute not only to your wealth but also to the vibrant tapestry of local economies.

Exploring Small Businesses as Wealth Generators

In the quest from $10,000 to a million, small businesses emerge as dynamic engines of wealth creation. This chapter unfolds the multifaceted

38

landscape of entrepreneurship, emphasizing the transformative potential of acquiring and nurturing small businesses.

The Entrepreneurial Canvas

Small businesses form the vibrant canvas of local economies, offering unique opportunities for astute investors. Unlike large corporations, these enterprises often present accessibility, agility, and untapped potential. Exploring this canvas becomes a strategic move for those aiming to multiply their initial investment.

Diverse Revenue Streams

Small businesses contribute to wealth generation through diverse revenue streams. Acquiring businesses that possess multiple income sources, whether through products, services, or licensing agreements, amplifies your potential returns. This diversification shields your investment from dependence on a single revenue channel, enhancing financial resilience.

Local Economic Impact

Investing in small businesses goes beyond personal wealth creation; it becomes a catalyst for local economic growth. These enterprises serve as pillars within communities, providing employment, fostering innovation, and contributing to the overall economic ecosystem. Your entrepreneurial endeavors have the power to uplift not only your financial standing but also the vitality of the regions you engage with.

Flexibility and Adaptability

Small businesses exhibit a remarkable ability to adapt swiftly to market changes. This inherent flexibility allows for rapid adjustments to consumer trends, technological advancements, and economic shifts. As an investor, aligning with businesses that showcase adaptability positions you to navigate the dynamic landscape of entrepreneurship effectively.

Potential for Scalable Growth

While small at inception, some businesses harbor immense potential for scalable growth. Identifying enterprises with untapped scalability becomes a key aspect of wealth generation. Strategic acquisitions can catapult these businesses to new heights, resulting in exponential returns on your initial investment.

Leveraging Existing Customer Bases

Acquiring small businesses often comes with the advantage of inheriting an established customer base. This pre-existing clientele provides a foundation for continued revenue, offering a head start in revenue generation. By effectively leveraging and expanding upon this customer base, you maximize the potential for sustained financial growth.

Paying Royalties to Local Owners

An innovative approach to small business acquisition involves paying royalties to local owners. This mutually beneficial strategy allows the original owners to continue benefiting from the success of the business while you, as the investor, receive a share of the profits. It fosters a collaborative and supportive relationship, aligning the interests of both parties towards shared financial prosperity.

Due Diligence and Risk Mitigation

Entering the realm of small business ownership necessitates thorough due diligence. Evaluating the financial health, market positioning, and growth potential of a business is paramount. Identifying and mitigating risks, whether related to operations, market dynamics, or internal challenges, safeguards your investment and sets the stage for sustainable wealth creation.

Negotiation Tactics for Acquisition

Successful small business acquisition requires adept negotiation tactics. From structuring favorable deals to aligning visions with the current owners, mastering the art of negotiation is crucial. This chapter provides insights into effective negotiation strategies, empowering you to navigate the intricate process of acquiring small businesses with confidence.

Strategic Management and Growth

Once acquired, strategic management becomes the linchpin of small business success. Implementing growth-oriented strategies, optimizing operations, and fostering innovation are integral to maximizing returns. The ability to envision and execute a strategic roadmap for business expansion positions you to unlock the full wealth-generating potential of these entrepreneurial ventures.

Building a Portfolio of Successful Ventures

The culmination of exploring small businesses as wealth generators is the assembly of a diversified and thriving portfolio of ventures. Each acquisition contributes not only to your financial growth but also to the mosaic of enterprises under your purview. A portfolio approach mitigates risk, leverages varied revenue streams and amplifies the collective impact on your journey to a million.

Envisioning Entrepreneurial Prosperity

In traversing the entrepreneurial landscape, envision a future where your acquisitions burgeon into flourishing enterprises, contributing not only to your wealth but also to the vitality of local economies. This chapter serves as a guide, illuminating the transformative potential of small businesses as formidable generators of wealth. Embrace the dynamism of entrepreneurship, and let your ventures paint a vivid picture of entrepreneurial prosperity on the canvas of your financial journey.

Acquiring Local Businesses and Paying Royalties

In the pursuit of $10,000 to a million, the entrepreneurial landscape beckons with innovative opportunities. This chapter unfolds the distinctive strategy of acquiring local businesses and introducing the concept of paying royalties—a synergistic approach that not only enhances your wealth but also fosters collaboration with local owners.

The Allure of Local Businesses

Local businesses, often the lifeblood of communities, present a unique appeal for investors seeking to make a meaningful impact. Acquiring these enterprises offers an opportunity to engage intimately with the fabric of a community, contributing to its economic vibrancy while strategically building your wealth.

Establishing Collaborative Relationships

Paying royalties to local owners represents a departure from traditional acquisition models. This collaborative approach involves sharing a percentage of profits with the original owners even after the acquisition. By establishing a symbiotic relationship, you align your interests with those of local entrepreneurs, creating a scenario where financial success becomes a shared endeavor.

Preserving Local Expertise and Insight

Paying royalties ensures that the knowledge and expertise of local owners are retained. Their familiarity with the community, customer preferences, and unique aspects of the business contribute to its ongoing success. This preservation of local insight not only bolsters the acquired business but also strengthens its roots within the community.

Community Engagement and Support

Engaging in royalty payments reinforces your commitment to the local community. As profits flow back to the original owners, the economic benefits extend beyond individual wealth creation. This model fosters community support, as residents witness a collaborative approach that sustains the businesses they cherish. It becomes a cyclical process of wealth creation and community upliftment.

Enhancing Local Economies

The acquisition of local businesses coupled with royalty payments becomes a catalyst for enhancing local economies. As these businesses thrive under new ownership, job opportunities increase, contributing to reduced unemployment rates. The injection of fresh ideas and resources amplifies the growth potential, making a positive impact on the economic landscape.

Building Trust and Goodwill

Paying royalties establishes a foundation of trust and goodwill within the community. It communicates a commitment to shared success and ensures that the transition of ownership is not perceived as a detachment from local values. This approach builds a positive reputation, paving the way for smoother operations and a more receptive community.

Financial Collaboration for Growth

The royalty payment model aligns the financial interests of both the new owner and the original business creators. It creates a collaborative environment where all parties are invested in the ongoing success of the business. This shared financial stake encourages strategic decision-making that prioritizes long-term growth, benefitting everyone involved.

Due Diligence in Royalty Arrangements

Effective implementation of royalty payments requires thorough due diligence. Clearly defined agreements, transparent communication, and legal documentation are essential components. Understanding the expectations of both parties, establishing royalty percentages, and addressing potential scenarios contribute to a solid foundation for this unique wealth-building strategy.

Strategic Acquisition Criteria

When acquiring local businesses with the intent of implementing royalty payments, strategic criteria should guide the selection process. Identify businesses with strong community ties, growth potential, and owners willing to embrace a collaborative approach. A harmonious relationship between the new owner and local entrepreneurs is

crucial for the success of this innovative wealth-building strategy.

Realizing the Vision of Shared Prosperity

The vision of acquiring local businesses and paying royalties extends beyond individual wealth creation. It embodies the spirit of shared prosperity, where financial success intertwines with community development. As you embark on this unique entrepreneurial journey, envision a future where the businesses you acquire become beacons of collaboration, nurturing both individual wealth and the collective well-being of the communities they serve.

Embracing the Future of Business Ownership

In exploring the strategy of acquiring local businesses and paying royalties, you step into the future of business ownership—one marked by collaboration, sustainability, and shared success. This chapter serves as a guide, illuminating the transformative potential of this approach and inspiring a vision where the local businesses you

acquire become enduring contributors to both your wealth and the vitality of the communities they call home.

Tips on Due Diligence, Negotiation, and Managing Acquired Businesses

Acquiring and managing businesses involves a multifaceted journey requiring astute due diligence, effective negotiation skills, and strategic management. This chapter offers practical tips to navigate each phase of this entrepreneurial endeavor, ensuring a comprehensive and successful approach to building wealth from $10,000 to a million through business acquisition.

Due Diligence Tips

1. Comprehensive Financial Analysis: Scrutinize the financial health of the business. Analyze profit and loss statements, balance sheets, and cash flow statements to gain a comprehensive understanding of its financial standing.

2. Legal Scrutiny: Engage legal professionals to review contracts, agreements, and any potential legal liabilities. Ensure compliance with regulations and uncover any legal risks associated with the business.

3. Customer and Vendor Relationships: Assess the strength of existing customer and vendor relationships. Understanding the reputation and satisfaction levels of stakeholders is crucial for post-acquisition continuity.

4. Operational Assessment: Dive deep into operational processes. Identify inefficiencies, evaluate supply chain dynamics, and assess the scalability of the business to ensure it aligns with your growth objectives.

5. Employee Analysis: Understand the skill set and morale of existing employees. A smooth transition post-acquisition often hinges on the retention and motivation of key personnel.

6. Market Research: Conduct market research to evaluate the business's competitive positioning. Understand market trends, customer preferences, and potential growth opportunities.

Negotiation Strategies

- Define Clear Objectives: Clearly articulate your objectives and desired outcomes before entering negotiations. Understanding your priorities enables strategic decision-making during the negotiation process.

- Establish Rapport: Build a positive relationship with the current owners. Establishing rapport fosters goodwill and can contribute to a smoother negotiation process.

- Flexible Approach: Be flexible but know your limits. While being open to compromises, identify non-negotiable aspects that align with your long-term vision for the business.

- Value Proposition: Communicate the value you bring to the table. Highlight synergies, growth plans, and how the acquisition aligns with the current owner's goals.
- Thorough Understanding: Gain a deep understanding of the business, its challenges, and potential opportunities. This knowledge equips you to negotiate from a position of informed strength.
- Seek Professional Advice: Engage experienced negotiators or advisors who specialize in business acquisitions. Their insights can be invaluable in navigating complex negotiations.

Managing Acquired Businesses

1. Communication is Key: Open and transparent communication is crucial during the transition. Articulate changes, expectations, and the vision for the future to reassure employees, customers, and other stakeholders.

2. Retain Key Talent: Identify and retain key employees. Their institutional knowledge and expertise are valuable assets during the transition and beyond.

3. Implement Strategic Changes Gradually: If significant changes are necessary, implement them gradually to minimize disruption. A phased approach allows for better adaptation and reduces resistance.

4. Cultural Integration: If acquiring a business with a distinct culture, focus on a smooth integration. Understanding and respecting the existing culture fosters a cohesive environment.

5. Leverage Technology: Implement technology solutions to streamline processes, enhance efficiency, and integrate the acquired business into your existing operations seamlessly.

6. Performance Metrics: Establish clear performance metrics and key performance indicators (KPIs). Regularly monitor and

assess these metrics to gauge the success of the acquisition and identify areas for improvement.

7. Customer Retention Strategies: Develop strategies to retain existing customers. Maintain continuity in products or services while introducing enhancements that align with your overarching business strategy.

8. Adaptability and Flexibility: Be adaptable and flexible in your management approach. Unforeseen challenges may arise, and the ability to pivot and adjust strategies is crucial for sustained success.

Envisioning Business Success

As you embark on the journey of acquiring and managing businesses, envision a future where each acquisition contributes not only to your wealth but also to the growth and prosperity of the businesses and communities they serve. This chapter serves as a compass, offering practical tips to navigate the complexities of due diligence, negotiation, and effective management. Embrace the entrepreneurial spirit, and let each acquired business become a building block in your transformative journey toward financial success.

Chapter 4: The Power of Networking

Uncover the transformative potential of networking as a pivotal force in your journey from $10,000 to a million. This chapter explores the art of forging connections, participating in mastermind clubs, and leveraging relationships for financial growth. Delve into the dynamic realm of networking, where each interaction becomes a stepping stone towards unlocking opportunities, gaining insights, and accelerating your ascent to financial prosperity.

Networking as a Key Factor in Wealth Creation

In the pursuit of transforming $10,000 into a million, networking emerges as a dynamic force, propelling individuals toward unparalleled financial growth. This chapter unravels the profound impact of strategic networking, emphasizing its role as a key factor in wealth creation.

Building a Strategic Network

1. Diverse Connections: Cultivate a network that spans diverse industries and professions. Each connection brings a unique perspective and potential opportunities that may contribute to your financial journey.

2. Mastermind Clubs: Joining mastermind clubs provides a platform to engage with like-minded individuals. Collaborate, share insights, and tap into collective wisdom to gain a competitive edge in your wealth-building endeavors.

3. Industry Events: Attend industry-specific events to expand your network within your chosen field. Engaging with professionals, thought leaders and potential collaborators positions you at the forefront of industry trends.

4. Networking for Opportunities

5. Uncovering Investment Opportunities: Networking opens doors to potential investment opportunities. Discussions with fellow entrepreneurs, investors, and business owners may unveil ventures aligned with your financial goals.

6. Partnerships and Collaborations: Forge strategic partnerships through networking. Collaborating with others can lead to joint ventures, shared resources, and expanded business opportunities that contribute to your overall financial growth.

7. Access to Capital: Establishing connections with investors and financiers broadens your access to capital. Networking facilitates introductions to potential funders who may be interested in supporting your entrepreneurial or investment ventures.

Gaining Valuable Insights

1. Market Intelligence: Networking provides access to valuable market intelligence. Conversations with industry insiders and professionals offer insights into market trends, consumer behavior, and emerging opportunities.

2. Learning from Peers: Engage with individuals who have successfully navigated similar financial journeys. Learning from their experiences, challenges, and triumphs equips you with practical knowledge for informed decision-making.

3. Mentorship Opportunities: Networking creates avenues for mentorship. Establishing connections with seasoned professionals allows you to benefit from their guidance, enabling you to navigate challenges and make informed financial decisions.

Leveraging Personal Branding

1. Visibility and Credibility: Networking enhances your visibility within professional

circles, establishing credibility and trust. A strong personal brand attracts opportunities and positions you as a reputable figure in your chosen industry.

2. Word-of-mouth referrals: Positive relationships fostered through networking often result in word-of-mouth referrals. These recommendations can lead to lucrative opportunities and partnerships, contributing to your financial success.

3. Access to Resources: A well-established network provides access to valuable resources, whether in the form of expertise, knowledge, or tangible assets. Leveraging these resources optimizes your capabilities in wealth creation.

Navigating Challenges Through Network Support

1. Problem Solving: Networking offers a pool of diverse talents and perspectives. When faced with challenges, tapping into this

network provides alternative viewpoints and creative solutions to navigate obstacles.

2. Emotional Support: Building a network goes beyond professional connections—it involves forming relationships. In challenging times, the emotional support from your network becomes a crucial factor in maintaining resilience and focus on your financial goals.

Networking Etiquette

- Reciprocity: Foster a culture of reciprocity within your network. Offer assistance and support to others, creating a collaborative environment where mutual benefits contribute to overall success.

- Authenticity: Be authentic in your interactions. Authenticity builds trust and credibility, laying the foundation for meaningful and enduring relationships within your network.

- Consistent Engagement: Regularly engage with your network. Whether through events, online platforms, or one-on-one meetings, consistent engagement strengthens connections and keeps you top-of-mind within your professional community.

Envisioning Networking Success

As you embrace networking as a key factor in wealth creation, envision a future where each connection and interaction becomes a catalyst for financial prosperity. This chapter serves as a guide, illuminating the transformative potential of strategic networking and inspiring a vision where your network becomes an instrumental force in your journey from $10,000 to a million. Embrace the power of connections, and let each network interaction propel you closer to your financial goals.

Joining Mastermind Clubs for Personal Growth

In the quest for personal and financial transformation from $10,000 to a million, the concept of joining mastermind clubs emerges as a powerful strategy. These clubs, where like-minded individuals converge to share insights, collaborate, and collectively pursue personal and professional growth, become a dynamic catalyst in the journey toward financial prosperity.

The Essence of Mastermind Clubs

1. Collective Intelligence: Mastermind clubs harness the collective intelligence and diverse perspectives of their members. Bringing together individuals with varied experiences and expertise creates a pool of knowledge that far exceeds what one person could achieve alone.

2. Mutual Support: Members of mastermind clubs share a common objective—personal

and financial growth. The culture of mutual support within these clubs fosters an environment where individuals uplift and inspire one another to reach new heights.

3. Accountability: The structure of mastermind clubs often involves setting goals and being held accountable by fellow members. This accountability mechanism propels individuals to stay focused on their objectives, fostering discipline and commitment.

Networking Opportunities

1. Expanding Your Circle: Joining a mastermind club expands your network significantly. Interacting with diverse professionals, entrepreneurs, and experts exposes you to a breadth of perspectives, opening doors to new opportunities, partnerships, and collaborations.

2. Access to Mentors: Mastermind clubs often attract seasoned professionals and mentors.

Engaging with these individuals provides access to valuable guidance, insights, and mentorship that can significantly impact your personal and financial journey.

3. Collaborative Ventures: The collaborative environment within mastermind clubs creates a fertile ground for joint ventures. Shared goals and complementary skills among members may lead to the formation of partnerships that amplify the potential for financial success.

Accelerated Learning

1. Knowledge Exchange: Mastermind clubs facilitate the exchange of knowledge and expertise. Learning from the experiences of others accelerates your learning curve, allowing you to assimilate insights and strategies that may have taken years to discover independently.

2. Peer Learning: Peer learning is a cornerstone of mastermind clubs. Engaging in

discussions, sharing challenges, and brainstorming solutions with peers contribute to a dynamic learning process that propels personal and financial growth.

3. Exposure to Diverse Industries: Mastermind clubs often attract individuals from various industries. Exposure to diverse perspectives and industry-specific insights broadens your understanding, enriching your knowledge base and enhancing your decision-making capabilities.

Personal Development and Growth

1. Self-Reflection: Interactions within mastermind clubs encourage self-reflection. Hearing the experiences and perspectives of others prompts you to evaluate your own goals, beliefs, and strategies, fostering continuous personal development.

2. Emotional Intelligence: Mastermind clubs provide a platform to enhance emotional intelligence. Interacting with individuals

from different backgrounds hones your ability to understand and navigate diverse personalities, a crucial skill in personal and professional spheres.

3. Confidence Building: Sharing your own experiences and insights within the supportive environment of a mastermind club contributes to confidence building. The positive feedback and constructive input from fellow members reinforce your belief in your capabilities.

Overcoming Challenges Together

1. Collective Problem-Solving: Challenges are inevitable on the path to financial growth. The collective problem-solving approach within mastermind clubs allows members to draw on the expertise of the group, generating innovative solutions and overcoming obstacles more effectively.

2. Resource Sharing: Mastermind clubs facilitate resource sharing. Whether it's

knowledge, contacts, or practical advice, members willingly contribute resources to help each other navigate challenges and seize opportunities.

3. Perspective Shift: Engaging with diverse perspectives within the club encourages a shift in how challenges are perceived. Alternative viewpoints often unveil new approaches and strategies, offering fresh insights into overcoming hurdles.

The Dynamics of Effective Mastermind Clubs

1. Structured Meetings: Effective mastermind clubs often operate with structured meeting formats. Regular meetings with predetermined agendas create a focused environment for meaningful discussions and goal-setting.

2. Clear Objectives: Clubs with clear objectives and a shared vision enhance the overall effectiveness. Members united by

common goals work cohesively toward personal and financial success.

3. Inclusivity: A culture of inclusivity encourages active participation from all members. When everyone feels heard and valued, the collective energy of the group is maximized, leading to greater synergy and collaboration.

Tips for Maximizing Mastermind Club Membership

1. Clearly Define Goals: Clearly articulate your personal and financial goals before joining a mastermind club. This clarity ensures that your contributions and interactions align with your overarching objectives.

2. Active Participation: Actively engage in club activities and discussions. Your contribution adds value to the collective wisdom of the group, and active

participation enhances the depth of your learning experience.

3. Open-mindedness: Approach interactions with an open mind. Be receptive to new ideas, perspectives, and feedback from fellow members. Open-mindedness fosters a culture of continuous learning and growth.

4. Commitment to Accountability: Embrace the accountability structure within the club. Setting and committing to goals, and being transparent about progress, contribute to the success of both individual members and the group as a whole.

Envisioning Personal and Financial Success

As you embark on the journey of joining mastermind clubs for personal growth, envision a future where the collective power of the group propels you toward unprecedented personal and financial success. This chapter serves as a guide, illuminating the transformative potential of mastermind clubs and inspiring a vision where each interaction becomes a catalyst for your journey from $10,000 to a million. Embrace the collaborative spirit of these clubs, and let the collective energy of like-minded individuals accelerate your ascent to new heights of achievement and fulfillment.

Chapter 5: Guided Entrepreneurship

Embark on a guided entrepreneurial journey as a cornerstone in your quest from $10,000 to a million. This chapter unveils the transformative power of hiring a business startup coach, providing insights into the strategic guidance and accountability essential for navigating the complexities of entrepreneurship. Discover how a coach becomes a compass, steering you toward success and ensuring your entrepreneurial endeavors align with the trajectory of financial growth.

The Role of Mentors in Achieving Financial Goals

In the pursuit of transforming $10,000 into a million, the guidance of mentors emerges as a potent force. These seasoned individuals, with their wealth of experience and insights, play a pivotal role in shaping personal and financial success.

1. Knowledge Transfer:

Mentors bring a wealth of practical knowledge acquired through years of experience. Leveraging their insights equips you with a unique understanding of the nuances involved in wealth creation. Whether it's navigating investment strategies, identifying market trends, or understanding financial pitfalls, mentors provide a real-world education that accelerates your journey.

2. Strategic Decision-Making:

Making informed and strategic decisions is fundamental to achieving financial goals. Mentors serve as trusted advisors, offering guidance on critical decisions. Their seasoned perspective helps you navigate complex scenarios, avoid common pitfalls, and make decisions that align with your overarching wealth creation strategy.

3. Expanded Network:

Mentors often have extensive networks cultivated over their careers. By aligning with a mentor, you gain access to their connections, opening doors to opportunities, collaborations, and valuable insights.

Networking becomes a powerful tool in your financial arsenal, fostering connections that can significantly contribute to your success.

4. Emotional Support:

The journey from $10,000 to a million is riddled with challenges and uncertainties. Mentors provide invaluable emotional support, offering encouragement during difficult times. Their reassurance and perspective help you navigate setbacks, maintaining focus on long-term objectives even in the face of adversity.

5. Accountability:

Mentors serve as a source of accountability, ensuring that you stay on course with your financial goals. Regular check-ins and discussions create a framework where progress is monitored, goals are reviewed, and adjustments are made as needed. This accountability mechanism fosters discipline and commitment to the financial journey.

6. Skill Development:

Mentors guide not only in strategic decision-making but also in skill development. Whether it's honing entrepreneurial skills, mastering investment analysis, or refining negotiation tactics, mentors provide personalized guidance for skill enhancement. This continuous development contributes to your overall competency in wealth creation.

7. Risk Mitigation:

Understanding and navigating risks is inherent in wealth creation. Mentors, having traversed their paths, offer insights into risk mitigation strategies. Whether it's diversifying investments, identifying potential pitfalls, or developing contingency plans, mentors contribute to a comprehensive risk management approach.

8. Real-Life Case Studies:

Mentors often share real-life case studies from their experiences. These anecdotes provide practical insights into successful strategies and lessons learned from failures. Learning from their journeys allows you to apply these lessons to your financial endeavors, avoiding common pitfalls and optimizing your decision-making.

9. Goal Alignment:

Mentors help align your financial goals with broader life objectives. Their guidance ensures that your pursuit of wealth is harmonized with personal values and long-term aspirations. This holistic approach fosters fulfillment and purpose in your financial journey.

10. Continuous Learning:

The mentor-mentee relationship is a symbiotic one. Mentors, too, benefit from the exchange of ideas and perspectives. Engaging with a mentor fosters a culture of continuous learning for both parties, creating a dynamic partnership that evolves with changing circumstances and market dynamics.

Envisioning Success with Mentors:

As you embrace the role of mentors in achieving financial goals, envision a future where their guidance propels you toward unprecedented success. This chapter serves as a testament to the transformative impact of mentorship, inspiring a vision where each interaction with a mentor becomes a catalyst for your journey from $10,000 to a million. Embrace the wisdom, experience, and support mentors provide, and let their guidance shape a future where financial prosperity aligns seamlessly with your aspirations and values.

Benefits of Hiring a Business Startup Coach

Embarking on the journey from $10,000 to a million through entrepreneurship is a formidable task, laden with challenges and uncertainties. Amidst the complexities of starting and growing a business, the role of a business startup coach emerges as a transformative force. Here are the key benefits of enlisting the services of a coach on this entrepreneurial odyssey:

1. Strategic Guidance:

A business startup coach provides strategic guidance tailored to your specific venture. Their expertise in business development, market analysis, and strategic planning equips you with a roadmap for success. This strategic direction ensures that your efforts are focused on activities that align with your financial goals.

2. Objective Assessment:

Coaches bring an external and objective perspective to your business. Their impartial evaluation helps identify strengths, weaknesses, opportunities, and threats. This objective assessment is invaluable in refining your business strategy and addressing areas that may require improvement.

3. Customized Solutions:

Each business is unique, and a one-size-fits-all approach seldom suffices. A startup coach tailors solutions to your business's specific needs and challenges. This customization ensures that the guidance provided aligns seamlessly with your vision and operational context.

4. Accountability Partner:

The entrepreneurial journey can be isolating, and self-accountability is often challenging. A coach serves as a dedicated accountability partner. Regular check-ins and progress reviews create a framework where goals are set, milestones are tracked, and adjustments are made as needed, fostering a disciplined approach to business growth.

5. Skill Development:

Entrepreneurial success demands a diverse skill set. A startup coach identifies gaps in your skill repertoire and designs targeted development plans. Whether it's honing leadership skills, mastering financial management, or enhancing marketing acumen, the coach guides your skill development journey.

6. Networking Opportunities:

A well-connected startup coach often brings a network of contacts and resources. Leveraging these connections provides valuable networking opportunities, potentially opening doors to partnerships, collaborations, and mentorship. Networking becomes a strategic tool in accelerating your business growth.

7. Confidence Building:

Navigating the uncertainties of entrepreneurship requires confidence. A coach instills confidence by providing constructive feedback, acknowledging achievements, and offering encouragement during challenging times. This confidence-building dynamic is crucial for sustaining motivation and resilience.

8. Risk Mitigation:

Entrepreneurship involves inherent risks, and a startup coach assists in identifying and mitigating potential pitfalls. Their experience in risk management guides you in making informed decisions, minimizing exposure to potential threats, and creating a robust risk mitigation strategy.

9. Faster Learning Curve:

The learning curve in entrepreneurship can be steep, and mistakes can be costly. A coach accelerates the learning process by sharing insights gained from their own experiences. This knowledge transfer ensures that you benefit from proven strategies and avoid common pitfalls encountered by entrepreneurs.

10. Emotional Support:

The emotional rollercoaster of entrepreneurship is a reality. A startup coach provides a supportive environment where you can openly discuss challenges, frustrations, and concerns. This emotional support fosters resilience and mental well-being, allowing you to navigate the highs and lows of entrepreneurship more effectively.

11. Goal Alignment:

Aligning your business goals with your aspirations is crucial for sustained motivation. A startup coach facilitates discussions to ensure that your business objectives harmonize with broader life goals. This alignment fosters a sense of purpose, contributing to long-term commitment and fulfillment.

12. Continuous Improvement:

The startup landscape is dynamic, requiring constant adaptation. A coach instills a culture of continuous improvement. Through regular assessments, feedback loops, and strategic adjustments, the coaching relationship becomes a dynamic process of refining and optimizing your entrepreneurial approach.

Envisioning Business Success with a Coach:

As you embrace the benefits of hiring a business startup coach, envision a future where your entrepreneurial endeavors thrive under the strategic guidance and support provided. This chapter serves as a testament to the transformative impact of coaching, inspiring a vision where each interaction with a coach becomes a catalyst for your journey from $10,000 to a million. Embrace the wisdom, expertise, and partnership that a startup coach brings, and let their guidance shape a future where business success aligns seamlessly with your financial aspirations.

Insights on Finding the Right Coach and Maintaining a Successful Coaching Relationship

Embarking on the journey from $10,000 to a million with a business startup coach is a strategic decision that can significantly impact your entrepreneurial success. The effectiveness of the coaching relationship hinges on finding the right coach and cultivating a dynamic and collaborative partnership. Here are key insights to consider:

1. Define Your Goals and Needs:

Before seeking a coach, clarify your business goals and identify the specific areas where you need support. Understanding your needs ensures that you can align with a coach whose expertise and coaching style complement your objectives.

2. Look for Industry-Relevant Experience:

The right coach should possess industry-relevant experience or have successfully coached entrepreneurs in similar sectors. This familiarity with the intricacies of your industry enhances their ability to provide tailored guidance and insights specific to your business landscape.

3. Assess Coaching Style and Approach:

Coaches employ different coaching styles and approaches. Some may be more directive, providing specific guidance, while others adopt a more facilitative approach, encouraging self-discovery. Assessing coaching styles helps you find a coach whose approach resonates with your preferred learning and decision-making style.

4. Seek Recommendations and Reviews:

Word-of-mouth recommendations and reviews provide valuable insights into a coach's effectiveness. Reach out to fellow entrepreneurs, business associates, or industry networks for recommendations. Online reviews and testimonials can also offer a glimpse into the coach's track record and the impact they've had on others.

5. Compatibility and Chemistry:

A successful coaching relationship thrives on compatibility and chemistry between the coach and the entrepreneur. Arrange an initial meeting or consultation to gauge the compatibility of personalities, communication styles, and overall rapport. A strong connection enhances the effectiveness of the coaching dynamic.

6. Clarify Expectations:

Open communication is crucial in any coaching relationship. Clearly articulate your expectations and discuss the coach's expectations as well. Establishing a mutual understanding of goals, timelines, and the overall coaching process lays the foundation for a collaborative and effective partnership.

7. Evaluate Problem-Solving and Listening Skills:

A proficient coach possesses strong problem-solving skills and active listening abilities. Evaluate how well the coach listens to your challenges, understands your perspectives, and collaboratively develops solutions. Effective problem-solving skills are essential for guiding you through various entrepreneurial hurdles.

8. Assess Commitment and Availability:

Ensure that the coach is committed to your success and has the availability to provide the support you need. Discuss scheduling, frequency of sessions, and the coach's availability for additional support when required. A coach who is genuinely invested in your success will prioritize your coaching relationship.

9. Monitor Progress and Adaptability:

A successful coaching relationship involves continuous monitoring of progress and adaptability to changing circumstances. Regular assessments of goals, milestones, and adjustments to the coaching approach as needed ensure that the coaching relationship remains dynamic and aligned with evolving business needs.

10. Open and Honest Communication:

Transparent and open communication is the cornerstone of a successful coaching relationship. Share your challenges, aspirations, and concerns openly with your coach. A coach who fosters a safe and open communication environment facilitates deeper insights and more effective collaboration.

11. Embrace Feedback:

Feedback is a valuable tool for growth. Be open to receiving feedback from your coach and, in turn, provide constructive feedback on the coaching process. This reciprocal exchange enhances the quality of the coaching relationship and contributes to ongoing improvement.

12. Assess Return on Investment:

Evaluate the return on investment (ROI) of the coaching relationship. Assess not only financial outcomes but also the personal and professional growth achieved through coaching. A coach who adds measurable value to your entrepreneurial journey enhances the overall ROI.

Envisioning Success with the Right Coach:

As you navigate the process of finding the right coach and cultivating a successful coaching relationship, envision a future where the guidance and support provided contribute significantly to your journey from $10,000 to a million. This chapter serves as a guide, inspiring a vision where the coaching relationship becomes a catalyst for entrepreneurial success. Embrace the insights shared, and let the coaching dynamic shape a future where your business aspirations align seamlessly with the guidance and expertise of a trusted coach.

Chapter 6: Putting It All Together

In the final chapter, synthesize the wisdom gained from paying off debts, real estate ventures, entrepreneurial pursuits, networking, and coaching. This chapter serves as a roadmap, guiding you in integrating these diverse strategies into a cohesive plan for transforming $10,000 into a million. Uncover the synergies between debt reduction, strategic investments, and the power of networks, crystallizing a comprehensive approach. Embrace the insights garnered from mentors, coaches, and collaborative ventures, propelling you toward financial success. Assemble the puzzle pieces of your financial journey, creating a unified vision that propels you confidently into a future of abundance.

Integrating Strategies for Holistic Wealth Creation

As you embark on the transformative journey from $10,000 to a million, the integration of diverse strategies becomes the linchpin for holistic wealth creation. This chapter unravels the art of seamlessly weaving together the insights gained from paying off debts, real estate ventures, entrepreneurial pursuits, networking endeavors, and coaching relationships, creating a comprehensive tapestry of financial success.

1. Debt Reduction as the Foundation:

Initiate your wealth creation journey by solidifying the foundation—paying off high-interest debts. As you reduce financial burdens, allocate freed-up resources towards strategic investments, providing a springboard for sustainable growth.

2. Real Estate Ventures for Long-Term Growth:

Leverage the power of real estate as a cornerstone in your wealth creation strategy. Purchasing a primary residence with a 3% down payment serves dual purposes—establishing a home and laying the groundwork for potential appreciation. Navigate the real estate landscape with a discerning eye, selecting properties with the potential for long-term growth.

3. Entrepreneurial Pursuits Guided by Coaches and Mentors:

Embark on entrepreneurial ventures with strategic guidance from coaches and mentors. The insights garnered from a business startup coach and industry mentors serve as invaluable compasses, steering your business endeavors toward success. Apply lessons learned from small business acquisitions, paying royalties, and effective management to cultivate thriving ventures.

4. Networking for Opportunities and Collaboration:

Networking is not just a singular pursuit; it's a thread woven throughout your wealth creation tapestry. Join mastermind clubs to amplify your network, creating opportunities for collaborations, partnerships, and shared ventures. The expansive connections fostered through networking become integral assets in your entrepreneurial and investment pursuits.

5. Mentorship as a Pillar of Wisdom:

Mentorship emerges as a pillar of wisdom, guiding your decisions and strategies. The relationship with mentors extends beyond individual ventures, offering overarching insights that shape your approach to wealth creation. Draw on their experiences, benefiting from the collective wisdom gained over years of navigating the complexities of business and finance.

6. Continuous Learning and Adaptability:

Weave a thread of continuous learning throughout your financial journey. Embrace adaptability, incorporating newfound knowledge and insights into your evolving strategy. The ability to pivot, refine, and innovate positions you to navigate changing market dynamics, ensuring resilience and sustained growth.

7. Balancing Risk and Opportunity:

Holistic wealth creation involves a delicate balance between risk and opportunity. Apply due diligence in assessing potential investments, considering the counsel of mentors and coaches. As you explore entrepreneurial ventures and investments, maintain a strategic equilibrium that aligns with your risk tolerance and long-term objectives.

8. Emotional Resilience and Accountability:

Infuse emotional resilience into the fabric of your wealth-creation journey. Accountability fostered through relationships with mentors, coaches, and networking connections, becomes the stabilizing force. Regular check-ins, goal-setting, and transparent communication ensure that you stay the course, even in the face of challenges.

9. Personal Growth as a Driving Force:

Holistic wealth creation transcends financial metrics; it encompasses personal growth and fulfillment. Assemble a mosaic that reflects your values, aligning your financial pursuits with broader life goals. Envision success not only as a numerical achievement but as a holistic manifestation of prosperity in various aspects of your life.

10. Visionary Integration for Future Success:

In weaving these strategies together, envision a tapestry that extends into the future—a future where your financial success is not only achieved but sustained and amplified. The integration of diverse strategies creates a resilient and dynamic approach to wealth creation, positioning you to navigate uncertainties and seize opportunities on the path to a million.

Embrace the Integrated Vision:

As you contemplate the integration of these strategies, envision a future where each element contributes to a harmonious and holistic wealth creation journey. This chapter serves as a guide, inspiring a vision where the integration of debt reduction, real estate ventures, entrepreneurial pursuits, networking, and coaching relationships becomes the catalyst for your transformation. Embrace this integrated vision, and let it guide you confidently into a future where abundance is not just a destination but a continuous and evolving journey.

Developing a Personalized Financial Plan

Embarking on the journey from $10,000 to a million requires not just a roadmap but a meticulously crafted and personalized financial plan. This plan serves as your compass, guiding each financial decision and strategic move with purpose. Here's a comprehensive guide to developing a personalized financial plan tailored to your unique circumstances and aspirations.

1. Clarify Your Financial Goals:

Start by articulating your short-term and long-term financial goals. Whether it's debt reduction, real estate acquisition, business growth, or investment milestones, clarity on your objectives is paramount. Each goal becomes a waypoint on your journey, informing the direction of your financial plan.

2. Assess Your Current Financial Position:

Conduct a thorough assessment of your current financial situation. This includes analyzing income, expenses, assets, and liabilities. Understanding your financial baseline provides insights into areas for improvement and opportunities for strategic investments.

3. Budgeting for Strategic Allocation:

Craft a detailed budget that allocates resources strategically. Prioritize debt repayment, allocate funds for investments, and earmark resources for savings and emergency funds. A well-structured budget becomes the tactical framework for executing your financial plan.

4. Debt Reduction Strategies:

If applicable, implement targeted strategies for debt reduction. Prioritize high-interest debts and explore consolidation options. Allocate a portion of your budget to consistently pay down debts, freeing up resources for wealth-building initiatives.

5. Real Estate Investment Planning:

For those venturing into real estate, outline a clear investment plan. Define criteria for property selection, establish budgetary constraints, and explore financing options. Integrating real estate into your financial plan involves a meticulous analysis of potential returns, property appreciation, and long-term value.

6. Entrepreneurial Ventures and Business Growth:

If entrepreneurship is part of your strategy, develop a business plan. Define your business model, target market, revenue streams, and growth projections. A well-crafted business plan serves as the blueprint for navigating the challenges and opportunities inherent in entrepreneurial endeavors.

7. Investment Diversification:

Craft a diversified investment strategy that aligns with your risk tolerance and financial goals. Explore various investment vehicles, such as stocks, bonds, mutual funds, and retirement accounts. Diversification minimizes risk and maximizes potential returns, contributing to a resilient financial portfolio.

8. Networking and Relationship Building:

Incorporate networking as an ongoing strategy within your financial plan. Attend industry events, join mastermind clubs, and foster relationships with mentors. Networking not only opens doors to opportunities but also enriches your knowledge base and positions you at the forefront of industry trends.

9. Coaching and Mentorship Integration:

Integrate coaching and mentorship relationships into your plan for ongoing personal and professional growth. Leverage the guidance of experienced individuals to refine your strategies, navigate challenges, and gain valuable insights that accelerate your journey to financial success.

10. Periodic Review and Adjustment:

A dynamic financial plan is not static; it evolves with changing circumstances and goals. Schedule periodic reviews to assess progress, evaluate the effectiveness of strategies, and make adjustments as needed. Flexibility ensures that your plan remains relevant and responsive to the dynamic nature of financial landscapes.

11. Emergency Preparedness:

Incorporate emergency preparedness into your financial plan. Establish an emergency fund to cover unforeseen expenses and mitigate financial shocks. A robust emergency fund provides a safety net, preventing unexpected challenges from derailing your overall financial strategy.

12. Aligning Personal Values and Financial Objectives:

Ensure that your financial plan aligns with your values and long-term aspirations. A plan rooted in your values fosters a sense of purpose and fulfillment. Holistic success extends beyond financial metrics to encompass a life that reflects your vision and values.

13. Continuous Learning and Adaptability:

Integrate continuous learning as a fundamental element of your financial plan. Stay informed about market trends, industry developments, and evolving investment strategies. Embrace adaptability, adjusting your plan based on new insights and changing circumstances.

14. Celebrate Milestones and Successes:

Acknowledge and celebrate milestones and successes along the way. Recognizing achievements, no matter how small reinforces motivation and provides positive reinforcement for staying committed to your financial plan.

15. Visionary Visualization of Success:

Visualize success as an integral part of your financial plan. Envision the realization of your goals, the growth of your investments, and the flourishing of your entrepreneurial ventures. This visionary component fuels motivation and fosters a mindset conducive to achieving financial milestones.

Embrace the Journey:

As you meticulously develop and implement your personalized financial plan, embrace the journey. Your plan is not just a series of financial strategies but a dynamic and evolving blueprint for achieving your aspirations. Each decision, each goal attained, and each obstacle overcome becomes a thread in the rich tapestry of your journey from $10,000 to a million. Commit to your plan, adapt as needed, and let it guide you confidently toward a future of financial abundance.

Balancing Risk and Reward in Investments

Investing is an art that involves navigating the delicate equilibrium between risk and reward. As you embark on the journey from $10,000 to a million, mastering this balance becomes paramount for achieving sustainable financial growth. Here's a comprehensive guide on how to navigate the intricate dance between risk and reward in your investment strategy.

1. Risk Tolerance Assessment:

Understanding your risk tolerance is the foundational step. Assess your comfort level with risk, considering factors such as financial goals, time horizon, and personal temperament. A realistic appraisal of your risk tolerance forms the basis for crafting an investment portfolio that aligns with your comfort level.

2. Diversification:

Diversification is a cornerstone in managing risk. Spread your investments across different asset classes, industries, and geographic regions. A well-diversified portfolio helps mitigate the impact of poor-performing assets, safeguarding your overall investment against market volatility.

3. Asset Allocation:

Strategically allocate your assets based on your financial goals and risk tolerance. A balanced mix of stocks, bonds, and other investment instruments provides a dynamic foundation. Adjusting asset allocation as market conditions and your financial objectives evolve ensures an adaptive and risk-aware investment strategy.

4. Research and Due Diligence:

Thorough research is a potent tool for managing risk. Conduct due diligence on potential investments, analyzing historical performance, market trends, and the underlying factors influencing each investment. Informed decisions based on comprehensive research enhance your ability to assess and mitigate risks effectively.

5. Risk-Reward Ratio:

Evaluate the risk-reward ratio for each investment. Assess the potential returns against the associated risks. A favorable risk-reward ratio ensures that the potential gains align with the level of risk you are willing to undertake. Striking a balance between risk and reward is key to optimizing your investment portfolio.

6. Long-Term Perspective:

Adopting a long-term perspective is a powerful strategy for managing risk. Volatility is inherent in financial markets, but a long-term horizon allows you to ride out short-term fluctuations. This patient approach minimizes the impact of market downturns, providing ample time for investments to recover and thrive.

7. Emergency Fund Preparation:

Maintain an emergency fund as a safety net. A robust financial cushion safeguards your investments from the need for premature liquidation during unexpected expenses. Having liquidity in reserve allows you to weather short-term financial storms without compromising your long-term investment strategy.

8. Stay Informed and Adaptive:

Market conditions and economic landscapes are dynamic. Stay informed about industry trends, geopolitical developments, and global economic shifts. Being adaptive and responsive to changing circumstances allows you to proactively manage risks and capitalize on emerging opportunities.

9. Professional Guidance:

Engage with financial professionals for expert guidance. Financial advisors and investment experts can provide insights into market conditions, risk management strategies, and tailored advice based on your unique financial situation. Their expertise enhances your ability to make informed investment decisions.

10. Consideration of Macro and Micro Factors:

Balance your risk assessment by considering both macro and micro factors. Macro factors include broader economic trends and geopolitical influences, while micro factors encompass the specific attributes of individual investments. A holistic approach that integrates both perspectives ensures a comprehensive risk evaluation.

11. Risk Mitigation Strategies:

Implement risk mitigation strategies within your investment plan. This may include setting stop-loss orders, diversifying across sectors, or incorporating hedging instruments. A proactive approach to risk mitigation fortifies your portfolio against unforeseen challenges.

12. Regular Portfolio Review:

Conduct regular reviews of your investment portfolio. Periodic assessments allow you to rebalance, reallocate, and adjust your strategy based on changing market conditions and your evolving financial goals. A disciplined and systematic review process ensures that your portfolio remains resilient and aligned with your risk tolerance.

13. Learning from Mistakes:

Learning from both successes and mistakes is integral to refining your investment strategy. Analyze past investment decisions, identify the factors contributing to successes, and extract valuable lessons from setbacks. This continuous learning process enhances your risk management skills over time.

14. Psychological Preparedness:

Emotional resilience is a critical aspect of balancing risk and reward. Be psychologically prepared for market fluctuations and unforeseen events. A disciplined and unemotional approach to investment decisions prevents impulsive reactions and ensures rational responses to market dynamics.

15. Continuous Monitoring and Adaptation:

Investing is an ongoing process that requires continuous monitoring and adaptation. Regularly reassess your investment strategy in light of changing market conditions, economic trends, and personal financial goals. A dynamic and responsive approach ensures that your investment portfolio remains well-positioned for long-term success.

Embracing the Risk-Reward Balance:

As you navigate the intricate interplay of risk and reward in investments, embrace the journey with a balanced perspective. Balancing risk and reward is not a static endeavor but a dynamic and evolving process. Each decision, each adjustment, and each success contributes to the tapestry of your financial journey, guiding you toward the ultimate destination of turning $10,000 into a million. Commit to the principles of risk management, stay adaptive, and let the harmonious balance between risk and reward propel you confidently toward financial success.

Chapter 7: Sustaining and Scaling Wealth

In this concluding chapter, delve into strategies for sustaining and scaling your wealth transformation. Explore avenues for continued growth, risk management, and adapting to evolving financial landscapes. Uncover the secrets to preserving wealth and maximizing its impact, propelling you beyond the initial million-dollar milestone toward enduring financial success. Embrace the principles of sustainability and scalability, ensuring that your journey from $10,000 to a million is not just a singular achievement but a stepping stone to a legacy of lasting abundance.

Long-Term Strategies for Sustaining Wealth

Sustaining wealth over the long term requires a thoughtful and strategic approach that goes beyond initial financial milestones. As you transition from $10,000 to a million and beyond, consider these key strategies for ensuring the enduring success and preservation of your wealth.

1. Holistic Financial Planning:

Wealth sustainability begins with holistic financial planning. Continuously reassess your financial goals, revisit your budget, and adjust your strategies in response to changes in your life, the economy, and the investment landscape. A comprehensive financial plan serves as a dynamic blueprint for navigating the complexities of wealth management.

2. Diversification and Asset Allocation:

Maintain a diversified investment portfolio with a balanced asset allocation strategy. Regularly review and adjust your portfolio to align with your risk tolerance and long-term objectives. Diversification across different asset classes and geographic regions helps mitigate risks and enhances the resilience of your wealth in the face of market fluctuations.

3. Estate Planning:

Plan for the orderly transfer of your wealth through effective estate planning. This includes creating a will, establishing trusts, and designating beneficiaries. A well-structured estate plan not only ensures the seamless distribution of assets but also minimizes tax implications, safeguarding your wealth for future generations.

4. Tax-Efficient Strategies:

Optimize your wealth by employing tax-efficient strategies. Work with tax professionals to identify opportunities for minimizing tax liabilities. This may involve strategic timing of asset sales, taking advantage of tax-advantaged accounts, and staying informed about changes in tax legislation that may impact your financial situation.

5. Continued Education and Adaptability:

Stay informed about financial markets, investment opportunities, and economic trends. Continuous education is essential for making informed decisions and adapting your strategies to evolving circumstances. A proactive and adaptable approach positions you to seize new opportunities while navigating potential challenges.

6. Insurance and Risk Management:

Protect your wealth through comprehensive insurance coverage and risk management strategies. This includes life insurance, health insurance, property insurance, and liability coverage. Adequate risk management safeguards your wealth against unforeseen events and provides financial security for you and your family.

7. Philanthropy and Legacy Building:

Consider integrating philanthropy into your long-term wealth strategy. Establishing a charitable foundation or contributing to causes aligned with your values not only makes a positive impact on society but also contributes to a lasting legacy. Thoughtful philanthropy can be an integral part of wealth sustainability.

8. Regular Portfolio Review and Rebalancing:

Regularly review and rebalance your investment portfolio. Periodic assessments ensure that your investments remain aligned with your financial goals and risk tolerance. Rebalancing involves adjusting asset allocations to maintain the desired risk-return profile and adapt to changing market conditions.

9. Ongoing Professional Guidance:

Engage with financial advisors, accountants, and legal professionals for ongoing guidance. Regular consultations with these professionals provide valuable insights into changing financial landscapes, regulatory updates, and strategies for optimizing your wealth. Professional advice complements your efforts in building and sustaining wealth.

10. Lifestyle Management:

Manage your lifestyle in alignment with your financial objectives. Avoid unnecessary debt, live within your means, and make conscious decisions about expenditures. Lifestyle management ensures that your spending habits support your long-term wealth goals and prevent the erosion of accumulated assets.

11. Health and Wellness Investments:

Invest in your health and well-being as a strategic component of wealth sustainability. Health-related expenditures, preventive care, and a focus on overall well-being contribute to longevity and reduce potential healthcare costs in the long run. Prioritizing health enhances your ability to enjoy your wealth throughout your lifetime.

12. Strategic Philanthropy and Social Impact:

Integrate strategic philanthropy and social impact initiatives into your wealth sustainability plan. Identifying causes that resonate with your values and leveraging your resources for positive change not only contributes to societal well-being but also enhances your legacy and the impact of your wealth beyond financial metrics.

13. Crisis Preparedness:

Develop crisis preparedness strategies to mitigate the impact of unexpected events. This includes having emergency funds, contingency plans, and a proactive approach to managing potential financial crises. Being prepared ensures that your wealth remains resilient in the face of unforeseen challenges.

14. Community Engagement:

Engage with your community and establish meaningful connections. Building strong ties with the community fosters a sense of belonging and social responsibility. Active community engagement contributes to the sustainability of your wealth by creating a positive environment for personal and financial growth.

15. Continuous Evaluation and Adjustment:

Wealth sustainability is an ongoing process that requires continuous evaluation and adjustment. Regularly reassess your financial goals, update your strategies, and adapt to changes in the economic, regulatory, and personal landscape. A dynamic and flexible approach ensures that your wealth remains resilient over time.

Embracing Long-Term Wealth Sustainability:

As you integrate these strategies into your financial plan, envision a future where your wealth not only grows but endures for generations. Wealth sustainability is not just about the accumulation of assets; it's about creating a legacy that transcends financial metrics. Commit to a holistic approach, balance risk, and reward, and let your wealth become a lasting testament to your financial acumen and values.

Scaling Up from a Million to Further Financial Milestones

Once you've successfully navigated the journey from $10,000 to a million, the question becomes: How do you scale up from this milestone to achieve even greater financial heights? Scaling up involves strategic planning, prudent decision-making, and a commitment to continued growth. Here are key considerations for scaling up your wealth from a million to further financial milestones:

1. Strategic Investment Allocation:

Reevaluate your investment portfolio and strategically allocate assets to align with your new financial goals. As you scale up, consider diversifying into different asset classes, exploring opportunities in emerging markets, and adjusting your risk tolerance based on your expanded financial capacity.

2. Business Expansion or Entrepreneurial Ventures:

If you've been involved in entrepreneurial ventures, explore opportunities for business expansion or consider new ventures. Scaling up often involves strategic growth in existing businesses or exploring innovative ventures that leverage your expertise and resources.

3. Real Estate Expansion:

Leverage your financial capacity to expand your real estate portfolio. Consider acquiring additional properties, exploring commercial real estate opportunities, or venturing into real estate development. Real estate expansion can provide both diversification and potential appreciation.

4. Advanced Tax Planning Strategies:

As your wealth increases, engage in advanced tax planning strategies to optimize your tax efficiency. Explore tax-advantaged investment accounts, charitable giving for tax deductions, and other sophisticated strategies that align with your financial goals.

5. Philanthropy and Impact Investing:

As you scale up, consider increasing your philanthropic efforts. Establishing a philanthropic foundation, contributing to impactful causes, or engaging in impact investing can not only create a positive legacy but also provide opportunities for strategic wealth management.

6. Global Investment Opportunities:

Explore global investment opportunities to diversify your portfolio and tap into growing markets worldwide. International investments, whether in stocks, bonds, or real estate, can provide additional avenues for wealth growth and risk mitigation.

7. Family Office or Wealth Management Services:

Consider establishing a family office or engaging in wealth management services to streamline your financial affairs. As your wealth scales up, personalized financial management becomes crucial for effective decision-making, asset protection, and legacy planning.

8. Continuous Learning and Networking:

Maintain a commitment to continuous learning and networking. Stay informed about evolving market trends, financial instruments, and investment strategies. Networking with industry professionals and fellow high-net-worth individuals provides insights and potential collaboration opportunities.

9. Strategic Debt Management:

Evaluate opportunities for strategic debt management. While being cautious about debt, strategic use of leverage can amplify investment returns and facilitate larger-scale ventures. Assess debt options with favorable terms and align them with your overall financial strategy.

10. Legal and Estate Planning:

Revisit your legal and estate planning to ensure that it aligns with your scaled-up wealth. Engage with legal professionals to update your will, trusts, and estate plans. Comprehensive legal and estate planning safeguards your wealth and facilitates a smooth transfer to future generations.

11. Risk Management and Contingency Planning:

As your wealth scales up, prioritize risk management and contingency planning. Diversify assets to minimize concentration risk, implement risk mitigation strategies, and ensure you have contingency plans in place for unforeseen events that could impact your financial portfolio.

12. Family Governance and Succession Planning:

Establish family governance structures and succession plans. As your wealth grows, involving family members in decision-making and planning for the transfer of wealth to the next generation becomes crucial. Transparent communication and governance structures help preserve family harmony and financial legacy.

13. Alternative Investments and Private Equity:

Explore alternative investments and private equity opportunities. These may include venture capital, private equity funds, or direct investments in private companies. Alternative investments can provide diversification and higher potential returns, albeit with additional risks.

14. Lifestyle Management:

Review and adapt your lifestyle to align with your scaled-up wealth. Consider how lifestyle changes may impact your financial goals, and make conscious decisions to ensure that your spending habits support your long-term financial objectives.

15. Financial Advisory Team:

Build and maintain a robust financial advisory team. Engage with financial advisors, investment professionals, tax experts, and legal professionals to ensure comprehensive guidance. A multidisciplinary team provides expertise across various aspects of wealth management.

Embracing the Journey of Scaling Up:

Scaling up from a million to further financial milestones is a dynamic and exciting journey. Embrace the opportunities and challenges that come with increased wealth. Commit to ongoing strategic planning, stay adaptive to market dynamics, and leverage your resources for both personal fulfillment and impactful contributions to society. As you scale up, let your financial journey reflect not only your wealth but the enduring legacy you create for generations to come.

Encouraging Ongoing Personal and Financial Development

Achieving financial success is not just about reaching a specific monetary milestone; it's a continuous journey of growth and development. As you navigate from $10,000 to a million and beyond, fostering ongoing personal and financial development becomes instrumental for sustained prosperity. Here are key strategies to encourage perpetual growth in both personal and financial aspects:

1. Cultivate a Growth Mindset:

Embrace a growth mindset that thrives on learning and adaptability. See challenges as opportunities for growth, view setbacks as learning experiences, and remain open to acquiring new knowledge. A growth mindset fosters resilience and innovation, crucial elements for ongoing personal and financial development.

2. Lifelong Learning:

Commit to lifelong learning as a cornerstone of personal and financial development. Stay informed about industry trends, emerging technologies, and evolving market dynamics. Attend workshops, webinars, and educational events to continuously enhance your knowledge base and stay ahead in your field.

3. Set Ambitious yet Attainable Goals:

Establish goals that stretch your capabilities while remaining attainable. Ambitious goals drive continuous improvement and motivation. Break larger objectives into smaller, manageable steps, creating a roadmap for ongoing progress. Regularly reassess and adjust your goals to align with changing circumstances and aspirations.

4. Networking and Mentorship:

Engage in networking and seek mentorship to broaden your perspectives and tap into collective wisdom. Networking introduces you to diverse insights, potential collaborations, and new opportunities. A mentor provides guidance, helping you navigate challenges and providing valuable feedback for personal and financial growth.

5. Strategic Career Development:

Invest in strategic career development to enhance your professional skills and advance your career. This may involve pursuing advanced degrees, certifications, or specialized training. Position yourself for leadership roles and seek out opportunities for career growth that align with your long-term financial objectives.

6. Financial Education and Literacy:

Prioritize ongoing financial education and literacy. Stay informed about investment strategies, tax planning, and financial instruments. Financial literacy empowers you to make informed decisions, optimize your wealth management, and adapt to changing economic landscapes.

7. Continuous Health and Wellness Focus:

Recognize the symbiotic relationship between physical well-being and financial success. Prioritize health and wellness to sustain your energy, focus, and overall quality of life. Regular exercise, a balanced diet, and sufficient rest contribute not only to personal development but also to your ability to navigate financial challenges with resilience.

8. Regular Self-Assessment:

Conduct regular self-assessments to evaluate your personal and financial progress. Reflect on achievements, identify areas for improvement, and celebrate milestones along the way. Self-assessment provides clarity on your evolving priorities and serves as a compass for ongoing development.

9. Embrace Financial Challenges as Learning Opportunities:

View financial challenges as opportunities for learning and growth. Whether it's navigating market downturns, managing debt, or addressing unexpected expenses, each challenge presents a chance to develop resilience, financial acumen, and adaptive problem-solving skills.

10. Explore New Ventures and Opportunities:

Remain open to exploring new ventures and opportunities. This could involve diversifying your investments, starting a new business, or venturing into unconventional paths. Embracing change and stepping outside your comfort zone fosters creativity and resilience in the face of evolving financial landscapes.

11. Emphasize Emotional Intelligence:

Recognize the importance of emotional intelligence in personal and financial development. Develop self-awareness, empathy, and effective communication skills. Emotional intelligence enhances your ability to navigate relationships, negotiate effectively, and make sound decisions in both personal and financial realms.

12. Leverage Technology for Personal and Financial Growth:

Embrace technological advancements to streamline personal and financial processes. Explore digital tools for budgeting, investment tracking, and financial planning. Leverage technology to enhance productivity, stay connected with industry trends, and optimize your approach to personal and financial development.

13. Actively Seek Feedback:

Actively seek feedback from mentors, peers, and professionals in your field. Constructive feedback provides valuable insights into areas for improvement and opportunities for growth. Cultivate a mindset that values feedback as a catalyst for personal and financial refinement.

14. Attend Conferences and Seminars:

Participate in conferences and seminars related to your industry and areas of interest. These events provide opportunities to connect with experts, gain exposure to innovative ideas, and stay at the forefront of industry developments. Networking at conferences can lead to collaborations and partnerships that contribute to ongoing growth.

15. Embrace a Balanced Lifestyle:

Maintain a balanced lifestyle that supports both personal and financial development. Strive for harmony between work, leisure, and personal relationships. A well-balanced life fosters overall well-being, resilience, and sustained motivation for continuous growth.

A Holistic Approach to Ongoing Development:

Encouraging ongoing personal and financial development requires a holistic approach that integrates various elements of life. Embrace the journey as a continuous evolution, where each experience contributes to your growth. By cultivating a growth mindset, staying committed to learning, and embracing development opportunities, you not only achieve financial success but also create a fulfilling and purposeful life journey.

www.ingramcontent.com/pod-product-compliance
Lightning Source LLC
Chambersburg PA
CBHW071206290526
45796CB00008B/164